Siberian Cats

Kate Conley

Checkerboard
Library
An Imprint of Abdo Publishing
abdopublishing.com

abdopublishing.com

Published by Abdo Publishing, a division of ABDO, PO Box 398166, Minneapolis, MN 55439.
Copyright © 2016 by Abdo Consulting Group, Inc. International copyrights reserved in all
countries. No part of this book may be reproduced in any form without written permission from
the publisher. Checkerboard Library™ is a trademark and logo of Abdo Publishing.

Printed in the United States of America, North Mankato, Minnesota.
042015
092015

THIS BOOK CONTAINS
RECYCLED MATERIALS

Cover Photo: Photo by Helmi Flick
Interior Photos: Alamy pp. 9, 14–15, 17; Glow Images pp. 1, 5, 11; iStockphoto pp. 13, 19, 21;
    Photo by Helmi Flick p. 7

Series Coordinator: Tamara L. Britton
Editors: Megan M. Gunderson, Bridget O'Brien
Art Direction: Neil Klinepier

Library of Congress Cataloging-in-Publication Data

Conley, Kate A., 1977- author.
  Siberian cats / Kate Conley.
      pages cm. -- (Cats. Set 9)
  Includes index.
  ISBN 978-1-62403-814-3
  1. Longhair cats--Juvenile literature. 2. Cat breeds--Juvenile literature. I. Title.
  SF449.L65C66 2016
  636.8'3--dc23
                    2015005165

Contents

Lions, Tigers, and Cats 4

Siberian Cats. 6

Qualities 8

Coat and Color 10

Size 12

Care 14

Feeding. 16

Kittens. 18

Buying a Kitten. 20

Glossary 22

Websites 23

Index 24

Lions, Tigers, and Cats

Long ago during cold Russian winters, wild cats hunted in dark forests. Their thick fur kept them warm. Powerful legs helped them jump great distances. These cats would later be **domesticated** and called Siberians.

Siberian cats are part of the family **Felidae**. Every member in this family is a cat. Some are wildcats, such as lions and tigers. Some are tame, such as house cats. Despite their differences, they share many similarities.

All family Felidae members are hunters. They have sharp teeth and claws. Their long, sleek bodies are good for climbing. People first domesticated these cats about 3,500 years ago. Today, they are beloved pets. One beloved **breed** is the Siberian cat.

The Siberian cat

Siberian Cats

Siberian cats come from Russia. They are an ancient **breed**. Russians have adored them for hundreds of years. Farmers used the cats to keep mice away from grains. These cats also appeared in Russian children's stories as loving creatures.

Communists took control of Russia in 1917. They discouraged pets. Food was in short supply. There was not enough extra to feed pets. So, Siberian cats roamed wild in the streets, markets, and forests.

By the 1980s, Russians were once again allowed to own pets. Local people adopted the **feral** Siberians. The cats were beautiful, sweet, and playful. Their owners began taking them to cat shows. Siberians were quickly named Russia's national cat.

In 2013, the Siberian was named the CFA's eighteenth most popular breed.

The first Siberians arrived in the United States in 1990. They soon became popular. The **Cat Fanciers' Association (CFA)** registered them in 2000. They were awarded championship status in 2006. Today, they are popular pets around the world.

Qualities

Siberian cats are energetic and playful. They are good with young children and other pets. Siberians are also calm, easygoing, and curious. Whatever their owners are doing, Siberians want to be included.

Sometimes, Siberians act more like dogs than cats. They like to greet their owners at the door, often making a sweet chirruping sound. They can tell when an owner is feeling sad. They will bring a favorite toy to the person and snuggle.

Siberians have another important **trait**. They have low levels of FelD1. FelD1 is an **allergen** that causes most cat allergies. This means Siberians make good pets for people who are allergic to other cats.

Some Siberians like cat beds.
But, most prefer to sleep in bed
with their owners.

Coat and Color

Snuggly Siberian cats have long, thick coats. Their coats have three layers. The top layer is coarse and waterproof. The **undercoat** is **dense** and soft. In the winter, the coat is thick and full. In the summer, Siberians **shed**. The thinner coat keeps them cool.

Siberians come in many colors. The most common are brown, red, black, and white. Sometimes, Siberians are one solid color. Other times, the colors combine. For example, a red cat mating with a white cat may have orange and peach kittens.

Siberians also come in a variety of patterns. Calico Siberians have patches of color all over their bodies. Siberian tabbies have striped fur. Pointed Siberians have dark legs, tails, and faces. Sometimes pointed Siberians look like they are wearing masks.

With so many colors and patterns to choose from, Siberians can have 124 coat color variations!

Size

Siberians are large cats. They take five years to reach their full size. Adult male cats weigh between 12 and 16 pounds (5 and 7 kg). Females weigh between 8 and 12 pounds (4 and 5 kg).

A Siberian's body has a gentle, rounded look. Its head is a medium wedge with rounded edges. The eyes can be any color. The Siberian has rounded ears, but they look pointed if they have tufts. Its paws are also rounded and sometimes have tufts.

A Siberian is known for its thick fur. It has long hair around its neck, which makes a ruff. Its tail is also thick and bushy. This is useful in cold weather. A Siberian wraps its tail around its face and paws to stay warm.

The Siberian is built for power. Its back legs are longer than its front legs. The legs have thick bones and strong muscles. These **traits** make the Siberian a powerful jumper. Despite its large size, the Siberian is graceful when jumping and climbing.

A Siberian's ears and toes may have tufts, or a bunch of small hairs. These hairs would have protected its ancestors from harsh weather.

Care

A Siberian cat requires care just like other **breeds**. It needs to visit the veterinarian for checkups. The vet can make sure your cat is healthy. A Siberian also needs to get **vaccines**. And, it is important to **spay** or **neuter** the cat if it is not going to be bred.

A Siberian's coat requires special care. Its long, thick fur may become **matted**. To prevent this, it needs to be brushed weekly. A special brush can be purchased at pet stores. This makes the job easier.

Your Siberian needs other special supplies. These include water and food dishes. Your cat also needs a **litter box**, which should be cleaned every day.

Don't forget to buy your Siberian some toys. This breed loves to play!

Feeding

Siberians are active cats. If they are getting plenty of exercise, they will have big appetites. They will need plenty of fresh water every day. They will also need quality cat food to prevent **obesity**.

Cat food comes in three types. There are dry, moist, and wet foods. Most cats have a preference for a certain type. Wet food is often the favorite. It is soft and chewy. Wet food is closest to what wildcats eat.

A vet can help you choose a healthy cat food. One way to do this is by looking at the list of ingredients. **Protein** should be the first item listed. Cats need quality protein to keep their hearts, eyes, and other organs healthy.

If you have multiple pets, make sure each pet has its own dishes.

Kittens

A female cat can have kittens when she is close to one year old. Once a cat mates, she is **pregnant** for about 65 days. Then, she finds a warm, quiet place to deliver her kittens.

When a mother cat has babies, it is called kittening. She often has three or four kittens in her **litter**. The kittens are helpless when they are born. They cannot see or hear. Kittens rely on their mother's care.

When kittens are young, they drink their mother's milk. Most kittens are **weaned** when they are about eight weeks old. Then they begin to eat solid cat food.

Kittens eat often, usually three to four times a day. They eat a lot because they are growing. But they also need energy to play!

Buying a Kitten

People can adopt kittens from many places. They may get one at a shelter. Another option is a **breeder**. Breeders are often the source for Siberian kittens. Siberians are a new breed in the United States. So, it is uncommon to find them in shelters.

A Siberian kitten is ready to be adopted when it is between three and four months old. It is important to prepare before bringing a kitten home. For example, the kitten will need food made especially for kittens and a food dish.

Kittens also need a warm, soft bed for sleeping. Sometimes they like to cuddle with a small stuffed animal. It reminds them of their littermates. Like older cats, kittens need a **litter box** and a scratching post. You are now ready to welcome your new friend!

With proper care, your Siberian cat will live for 10 to 15 years.

Glossary

allergen - a substance that causes an allergy.

breed - a group of animals sharing the same ancestors and appearance. A breeder is a person who raises animals. Raising animals is often called breeding them.

Cat Fanciers' Association (CFA) - a group that sets the standards for judging all breeds of cats.

communist - a person who believes in communism. Communism is a social and economic system in which everything is owned by the government and given to the people as needed.

dense - thick or compact.

domesticated - adapted to life with humans.

Felidae (FEHL-uh-dee) - the scientific Latin name for the cat family. Members of this family are called felids. They include lions, tigers, leopards, jaguars, cougars, wildcats, lynx, cheetahs, and domestic cats.

feral (FIHR-uhl) - having gone back to the original wild or untamed state after being tame.

litter - all of the kittens born at one time to a mother cat.

litter box - a box filled with cat litter, which is similar to sand. Cats use litter boxes to bury their waste.

mat - to form into a tangled mass.

neuter (NOO-tuhr) - to remove a male animal's reproductive glands.

obesity - the condition of having too much body fat.

pregnant - having one or more babies growing within the body.

protein - a substance which provides energy to the body and serves as a major class of foods for animals. Foods high in protein include cheese, eggs, fish, meat, and milk.

shed - to cast off hair, feathers, skin, or other coverings or parts by a natural process.

spay - to remove a female animal's reproductive organs.

trait - a quality or feature of something.

undercoat - short hair or fur partly covered by longer protective fur.

vaccine (vak-SEEN) - a shot given to prevent illness or disease.

wean - to accustom an animal to eating food other than its mother's milk.

Websites

To learn more about Cats,
visit **booklinks.abdopublishing.com**. These links are routinely monitored and updated to provide the most current information available.

Index

A

adoption 20
allergens 8

B

bed 20
body 4, 10, 12
breeder 20

C

Cat Fanciers' Association 7
character 6, 8, 10, 16
claws 4
coat 4, 10, 12, 14
color 10, 12

E

ears 12
eyes 12, 16

F

FelD1 8
Felidae (family) 4
food 14, 16, 18, 20

G

grooming 14

H

head 10, 12
health 14, 16
history 4, 6, 7

K

kittens 10, 18, 20

L

legs 4, 10, 12, 13
litter box 14, 20

N

neuter 14

P

paws 12

R

reproduction 18
Russia 4, 6

S

scratching post 20
senses 18
shedding 10
size 12, 13
spay 14

T

tail 10, 12
teeth 4
toys 8, 20

U

United States 7, 20

V

vaccines 14
veterinarian 14
voice 8

W

water 14, 16